Delhi

by Joyce Markovics

Consultant: Karla Ruiz, MA
Teachers College, Columbia University
New York, New York

New York, New York

Credits

Cover, © Saiko3p/Shutterstock; TOC Left, © JTB MEDIA CREATION, Inc./Alamy Stock Photo; TOC Right, © Iryna Rasko/Shutterstock; 4–5, © yellowcrestmedia/iStock; 5B, © Hindustan Times/Newscom; 7, © hadynyah/iStock; 8, © Hung Chung Chih/Shutterstock; 9T, © BensonHE/Shutterstock; 9B, © saiko3p/Shutterstock; 10L, © INDWILD/Alamy Stock Photo; 10–11, © mountlynx/iStock; 12, © wildlywise/Shutterstock; 13, © Karunesh Johri/Shutterstock; 14–15, © Dinodia Photos/Alamy Stock Photo; 15R, © Swaminarayan Akshardham; 16, © AlpamayoPhoto/iStock; 17T, © Steve Davey Photography/Alamy Stock Photo; 17B, © Kaarthikeyan.SM/Shutterstock; 18, © MONEY SHARMA/EPA/Newscom; 19, © MONEY SHARMA/EPA/Newscom; 20L, © david pearson/Alamy Stock Photo; 20–21, © F9photos/iStock; 22 (Clockwise from Top Right), © Nikada/iStock, © imagedb.com/Shutterstock, © MOLPIX/Shutterstock, © MONEY SHARMA/EPA/Newscom, © wildlywise/Shutterstock, and © INDWILD/Alamy Stock Photo; 23 (T to B), © szefei/Shutterstock, © MOLPIX/Shutterstock, © Ali Arsh/CC BY 4.0, © Rudolf Tepfenhart/Shutterstock, and © RonTech3000/Shutterstock; 24, © Aleksandar Todorovic/Shutterstock.

Publisher: Kenn Goin
Senior Editor: Joyce Tavolacci
Creative Director: Spencer Brinker
Photo Researcher: Thomas Persano

Library of Congress Cataloging-in-Publication Data

Names: Markovics, Joyce L., author.
Title: Delhi / by Joyce Markovics.
Description: New York, New York : Bearport Publishing, [2018] | Series: Citified! | Includes bibliographical references and index. | Audience: Ages 5–8.
Identifiers: LCCN 2017014713 (print) | LCCN 2017015163 (ebook) | ISBN 9781684022915 (ebook) | ISBN 9781684022373 (library)
Subjects: LCSH: Delhi (India)—Juvenile literature.
Classification: LCC DS486.D3 (ebook) | LCC DS486.D3 M268 2017 (print) | DDC 954/.56—dc23
LC record available at https://lccn.loc.gov/2017014713

For more information, write to Bearport Publishing Company, Inc., 45 West 21st Street, Suite 3B, New York, New York 10010. Printed in the United States of America.

10 9 8 7 6 5 4 3 2 1

Contents

नई दिल्ली
NEW DELHI نئی دلّی
समुद्र तल से ऊँचाई MEAN SEA LEVEL 214·42 मी.Mtrs.

Welcome to

DELHI

The City of Rallies!

Delhi is the **capital** of India. Why is it called the City of Rallies? Large groups of people often gather, or rally, in Delhi's streets.

Delhi is a huge city in northern India.

It covers 573 square miles (1,484 sq km).

More than 20 million people call Delhi home.

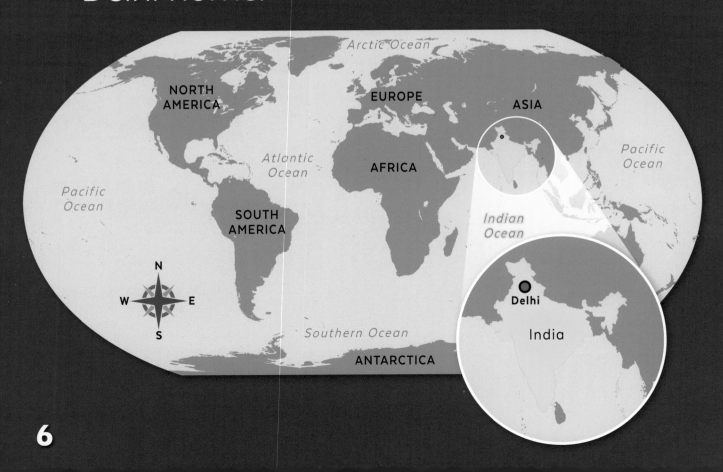

Delhi has two sections—
Old Delhi and New Delhi.

7

Delhi is a very old city.

It dates back thousands of years.

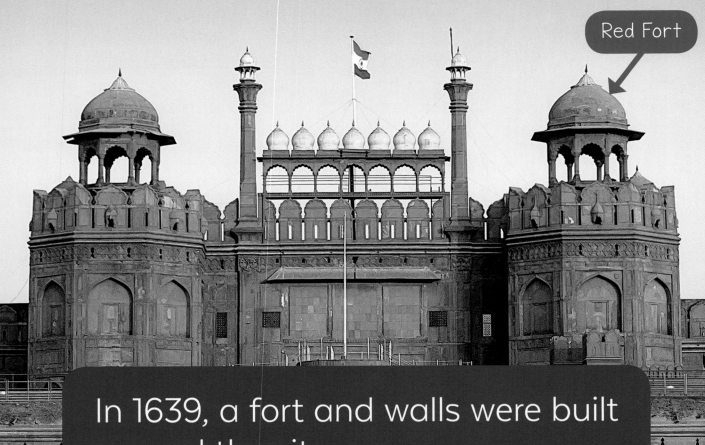

Red Fort

In 1639, a fort and walls were built around the city.

The huge walls kept enemies out.

8

Delhi has many modern buildings. This one looks like a lotus flower.

Did you know that much of Delhi is green?

Forests and parks cover more than 20 percent of the city.

One of Delhi's parks is home to a herd of wild deer!

Delhi has more than 20 parks.

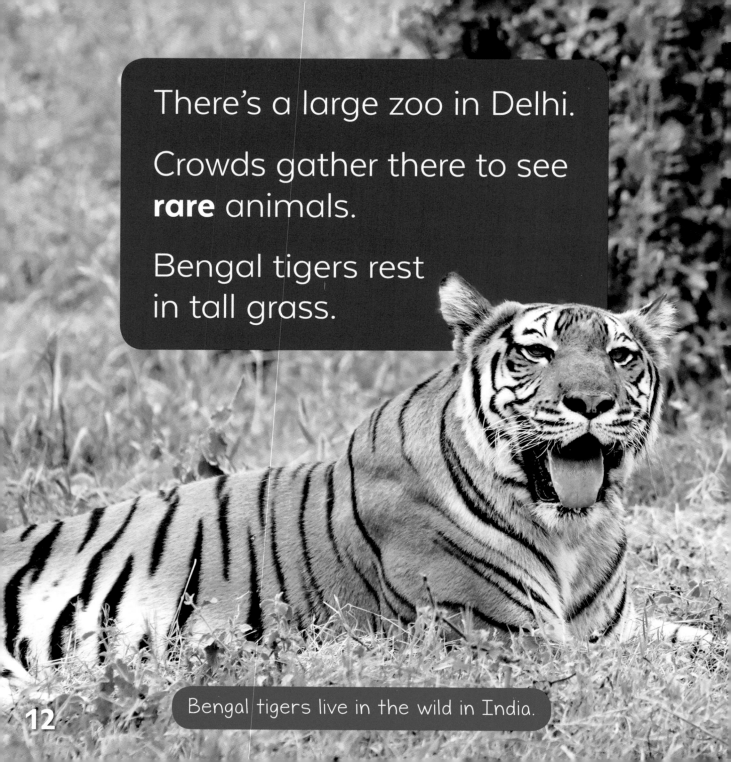

There's a large zoo in Delhi.

Crowds gather there to see **rare** animals.

Bengal tigers rest in tall grass.

Bengal tigers live in the wild in India.

Rhinos cool off in muddy pits.

There are more than 1,000 animals at the zoo.

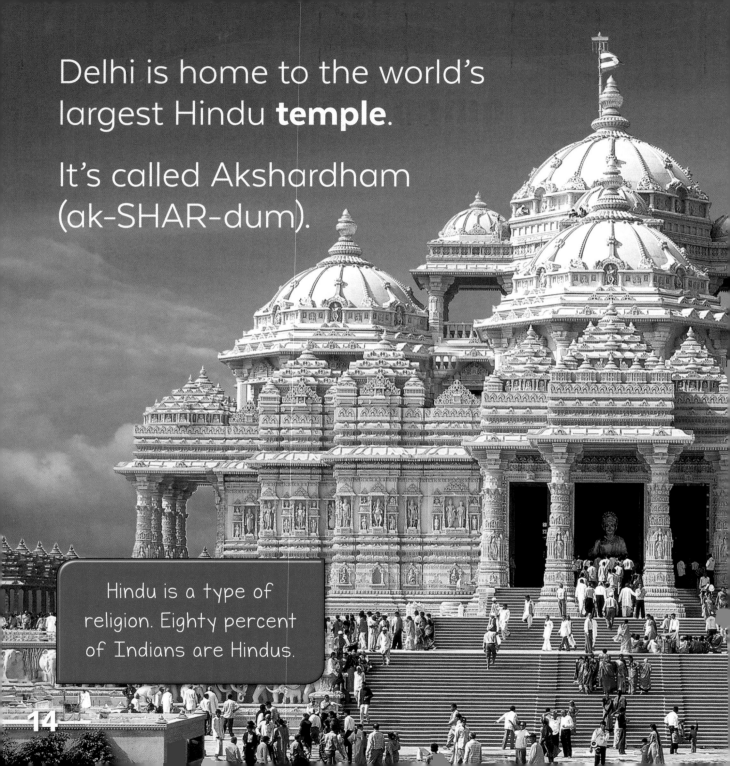

Delhi is home to the world's largest Hindu **temple**.

It's called Akshardham (ak-SHAR-dum).

Hindu is a type of religion. Eighty percent of Indians are Hindus.

The giant temple is built entirely out of stone!

It's covered with carvings, including 148 life-size elephants.

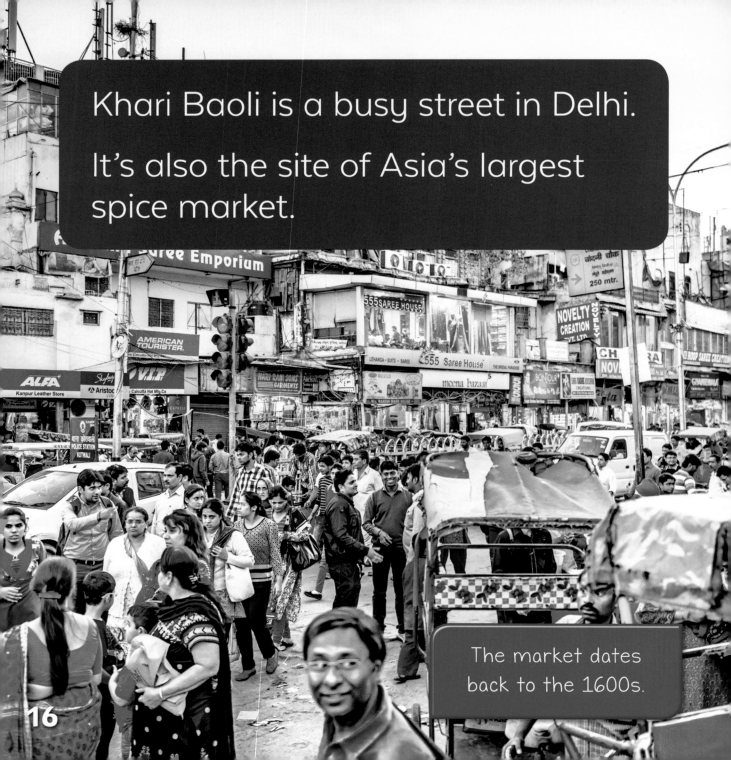

Khari Baoli is a busy street in Delhi.

It's also the site of Asia's largest spice market.

The market dates back to the 1600s.

Large bins of colorful spices and nuts line the streets.

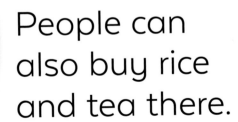

People can also buy rice and tea there.

What else is interesting about Delhi?

It's home to a toilet museum!

18

Many models are on display—
even a French one that looks
like a **throne**.

The throne toilet
is similar to one
used by France's
King Louis XIV
(1638–1715).

Beep, beep, beep!

People zoom around Delhi in three-wheeled cars.

They're called auto rickshaws.

They transport people all over the huge city!

In India, drivers sit on the right side of the car.

MAP IT!
Delhi

**Khari Baoli
Spice Market**

Akshardham

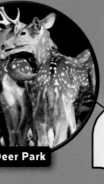
Deer Park

**National
Zoological Park**

Toilet Museum

Yamuna River

Cool Fact:
Delhi is home to the world's tallest brick **minaret**. It's called Qutub Minar and rises 239 feet (73 m)!

Qutub Minar

Glossary

 **capital** (KAP-uh-tuhl) a city where a country's government is based

 **minaret** (min-*uh*-RET) a tall, thin tower attached to a religious building called a mosque

 **rare** (RAIR) not often found or seen

 **temple** (TEM-puhl) a religious building where people go to worship and pray

 **throne** (THROHN) a chair used by a ruler

23

Index

Read More

Apte, Sunita. *India (True Books: Countries).* New York: Scholastic (2009).

Markovics, Joyce. *India (Countries We Come From).* New York: Bearport (2016).

Learn More Online

To learn more about Delhi, visit
www.bearportpublishing.com/Citified

About the Author

Joyce Markovics lives along the Hudson River in a very old house. India is the most amazing place she has ever visited.

Delhi